_____ Many Times, But Then _____

University of Texas Press Poetry Series,
NO. 4

Many Times, But Then

By Ann Lauterbach

University of Texas Press, Austin and London

LIBRARY OF CONGRESS CATALOGING IN PUBLICATION DATA

Lauterbach, Ann, 1942–
  Many times, but then.
  (The University of Texas Press poetry series; no. 4)
  I. Title.
PS3562.A844M3   811'.5'4   78-27309
ISBN 0-292-75046-3
ISBN 0-292-75047-1 pbk.

Permission to publish the following poems is gratefully acknowledged:
"Romance," *Partisan Review* 45, no. 1: 10. Copyright © 1978 by Partisan
      Review, Inc.
"A Visit to the Country," *Partisan Review* 43, no. 3: 407. Copyright ©
      1976 by Partisan Review, Inc.
"Gramercy Park Evening," "True and False Green," "After All,"
      "Connie's Window, Nantucket," *Roof* 2 (Spring 1977).
"Chalk," *ZZZ*, ed. Kenward Elmslie, copyright © 1974 by Z Press, and
      "Last Night it Rained," "January Hill," "Parabolas of
      Spring," *ZZZZZZ*, ed. Kenward Elmslie, copyright ©
      1977 by Z Press.
"September Solitaire," *Heresies* 2 (May 1977), p. 47.
"Single File," "Between," "The Day After," *Là Bas* 11 (March 1978).
"Second Descent: 1975," "True and False Green," "Alternating Articles,"
      "Tremors in a Late Age," "Chappaqua Reverie," "Words
      to Assuage," *Book One*, ed. Sal Incontro, copyright ©
      1975 by the Spring Street Press.
"Many Times, But Then," "Reynolda Gardens," "Along the Way," *Poetry
      in Motion*, no. 11, ed. David Lehman, 1979.
"Poem," "Quotations from Reality," *The Little Magazine* 11, no. 1
      (Spring 1977).
"Then Suddenly," *The Face of the Poet*, by Alex Katz. New York: Brooke
      Alexander, Inc., 1979.
"The White Sequence," "Configuration of One," *The Little Magazine* 10,
      no. 2 (Summer 1976).
"Gray Morning," *The New York Arts Journal*, no. 8 (February and March
      1978).
"Window," *The Nation*, April 2, 1977.
"Winter Sky," "East River Barge," *The Poetry Mailing List*, ed. and pub.
      Steven Paul Miller, New York, 1977.
"These," "Stories without Endings," Grey Art Gallery, New York
      University, New York, 1979.
"The Relinquished," *Stooge* 7 (May 1972).
"The Green Scarf," *Jazz4/Linguis* (April 1979).
"Gardenia," *The Poetry Project Newsletter*, no. 62 (February 1979).

for Priscilla
and for Tom Prideaux

Ought not these oldest sufferings of ours to be yielding
more fruit by now? Is it not time that, in loving,
we freed ourselves from the loved one, and, quivering, endured:
as the arrow endures the string, to become, in the gathering out-leap,
something more than itself? For staying is nowhere.

Rilke, *First Elegy*

Contents

If only it were a matter of wet strawberries
among wet lettuces, or the mauve gray haze
on the road north. The decors
rush in and we are sated by looking
but there are other colorations, other codes.
There were frogs all over the airport.
There was nothing around but France.
And there are the nights when a long caress
breaks through the film of sleep
yielding something unspeakably true.

I wanted to say, "All I want inside is you."
I did not, because you are not
all that I want. If I insist, and I do,
on always including you, it is because
I foresee no other anchor when things are
so windy and culpable. We must return to the day
we were shattered into care, even
with the severe things going on in front of us.

The bloom, stranded somehow in glass and a view
of marvelous, slow-moving things
nameless because I had run out of names.
Measures had to be taken.
But I had been to New Jersey and back
and hadn't even noticed the bridge.
Talk is a way of not looking.
But notice how he sits in his chair
without so much as a color on his mind
while at the same time light
accrues behind a mass of leaves. Now
everything is darker. I think she is on a cruise
in the Black Sea wearing her portrait
(how we see her, dream of her)
while at the same time worried about the farm.
She told me what comes to mind is
"then suddenly", an icon
for which she is never prepared but always knows.
I was trying to get at it, the way
it goes awkwardly forward on the pavement
until it takes hold, draws
out of the drive across the bridge
lights strung ahead in litanies of sudden knowledge.

1.

Now it moves towards declaration, I try
to embody the future
by changing my clothes over and over.
Finally: an old pink T-shirt
under the black Moroccan blouse,
elaborately stitched,
I bought for an occasion. And
I have changed my rings from silver
to gold.
            There are distractions:
the smell of toast up through floors
and the bunch of orange flowers
that will live to bridge the seasons.
The first snow is snowing in the midwest.

2.

One could always go to the Hebrides, or Kansas.
Anywhere where there is profuse
nothing, nothing but air in motion
and distances to boggle the imagination.
Or one could stay at home and count
all the white things as if searching
for the exception to a rule. A rule of thumb.
A rule of eye. A rule of heart. What
rules the heart?
          Dr. Johnson toured the Hebrides.
On Sunday he said, "It should be different
from another day. People may walk, but not
throw stones at birds. There may be
relaxation, but there should be no levity."

3.

What is it about? Skirting the issue
and such costumes as we found in the attic.
You know mother wore these
delicate dresses and you know how long ago
everything gets. Her mother
looked out the window and said
it was all yellow. It was all rose, but
white at the edge.
                    At the edge I stare
to keep from slipping, but it's clear
I cannot oppose this inwardness.
My great aunt was a painter. She
made delicate paintings of woodland scenes.
She is extremely old now and bites her nurse.

4.

Nothing speaks for itself. Why is this box
full of unwrapped gifts? The frog
has turquoise eyes and the bracelet is made
from carved ivory. Here is a hand
in the form of an ashtray. Someone
is saving up for something unexpected.

A rainy day? No, today is cold
and the sun is making forays onto brick.
The two white candles have never been lit
and the ivy is almost dancing
from thirst. One day
we walked far into the woods
and saw a dead tree which curved and curved.

5.

You wonder all the time
how you got there and invent
another life, past or future, by which
to come back. The dry things help.
Everything is essentially frail and brown.
The leaves are braille on the ground
and the sky is coming into permanent white.

Most of the people you know are almost mad.
You are mad and talk to yourself
as if you existed, wearing make-up
familiar as winter but always smiling.
The next time you will return as a clown
and speak only with gestures of gloved hands.

6.

How about simple exhaustion, like a crease?
After a while you run out of examples
and have to change course.
I think this is my last example.
Now I am free to roam, free
to join the singers on the road to Buffalo.
Tomorrow I will hire a van
and have it painted white
and wire it for sound
and line it with satin
and head out. I will invite no one.
It will be the first example of something else.
There is a rudimentary addition in life
and there is the need to subtract, or erase.

7.

I would not have waited gladly longer.
Today's design is clarity and height,
almost free of history. One night
we were almost free of history.
Each thing has that white on white
the way these bricks, hit by sun,
stop passage but still define it.

The flowers in the blue vase have died
but the leaves of the big plant
hold up luminosities, which change.
And tonight, the placemats imply
a literal possibility. As you come ·
to tell me what it is you are going
to tell me, I eye things for transience.

You are not obliged to answer; the requirements are lifted.
However, I have knelt, recently, to see
for the first time your hands
as if I had looked up, mid-summer, to see
the bird whose song I had missed.
Intensifications are hard to come by. We know this.
Now we are back among possibilities: drug stores, Mahler,
spice racks and these swivel chairs remaindered
for practically nothing. Houses burn
while we sleep in beds provided,
the real information changed to tone poems in Malibu,
portraits in New York. Seeing you after these years.
A cracked heart is mended with another cracked heart,
medallion with Pegasus on one side, Venus the reverse,
the winged horse who kicked a mountain and she,
didn't she walk out of the water as Virginia Woolf walked in?

Winter Sky

Add to what you already know
the fact that it is severely cold today
and add that to the difficulty of the literal
because the literal somehow misses
the way you can miss
the blue sky on a cold day.

But because it turns out
that life is essentially an old string
on which we bead beads, some of which match,
we cannot help but mention the same thing
over and over, as the sky mentions blue.

As for you, you
have probably taken it lightly, you
are so good at doling out events
that cause recollection, like that day
you pulled something across the future
and the sky was blue.

A friend wrote: "you know of course
the 'you' in that short piece I wrote
beginning 'I dreamed that you were in
my dream' etc. was you" and you know
last night I dreamed
someone had put a fine wire
across my path and I tripped:
and I told someone the reason I thought
I like green so much is because
I was once a bird. "An owl," he said.
Some people have said I was
in Italy during the time of the Medicis
but I think it was earlier, back
when Giotto was pressing angels
into flat chapel walls. When you came
into the room last night I was that again.

All these balloons hovering. No wind.
First thing in the morning when
this repeats that, not yet
invaded by frozen foods although
the peas are intensely green
just like the balloons.
                              And the one lost marble
is also green, its dusty circumference
stuck far under the radiator
remote as architecture.
                              Unseasonably mild.
Now Bette Davis struts out
a wounded witch or a lame mechanical bird
angular with contempt. My hip blocks the view.
I hear you hate words because they color the truth.

The white anemone faints for a second time,
the white anemone faints again. It is
a refrain, behind me, in water.
Across the white floor a white anemone
has fainted. I am not remembering
and when you are part of what I say
it is not you I am remembering.

At last we are on vacation in Italy.
Where are you from? I remember.
Touching the pink table, a stem
loops down. The white anemone has fallen.
A flower collapsed on the pink ground. It
happened recently. I do not remember when.

Gray Morning

There are oils that slip us out of place
and we are too far away to believe in anything, much less
the nearness of the singular. You, asleep, aside,
crouch by a river watching slivers collide.
The heat is unbearable, the air
carries nothing back from the coast except birds
which are always present like a vivid, extreme desire.
Did you ever climb the mountain? I stare
where we were, where there is nothing to look for.

Meanwhile, cups are loose in grades of gray.
Decisions must be made between pearl and mercury,
shades of meaning only painters know, as only painters
see ingredients. How will green yield to pearl
or yellow hang on mercury? There is always color
where the body lay; not the dream, but its impact.
The names of things accost us as we wake.

Where are you? I don't care. I care
how you look as you get up to go, in search of the thing
you think you miss. What you see in the distance
never gets close, the allure
of slender reeds and girls, of blue jackets and pearls,
an inventory of images by which we make ourselves real.
You move from the water, altogether far.
Light ventures the window and touches down, profusely near.

Window

The distance between heat and cold
a window's width, glass light
held by an incursion
the way love is always shadowed.
In the beginning I reached
as if stricken by the need to follow
but you were afterwards afraid.
Now I am trying to figure out how far
you went, knowing it is winter
and a long stretch before the air
moves in and out at room temperature.

Chalk

Moon marked sky; sky writings.
Trace of birds, of egg white
and faeces of fish;
bone powder
of sea gulls and heron wings.
Shells fluted and difficult.

Noon on black sea
broken on cliffs; wet
erasure, night pavements
chalked with directions.

The moist residue of sex
dries chalk.

Music chalks air.
Dust on bowstrings, hair
of the horse breathing the cold
chalk breath in its lungs.

The extension of fingers;
an intensity of veils.
Salt settled on skin.
Transparencies of love
caked on the hearts of the old.

The arrival of winter is chalk.
The thing recalled is chalk.

The Golden Goose turned to chalk.
Rome is chalk
and Leda's swan.
The breasts of Venus are chalk.

The aftermath of dance
is patterns of chalk on sand—
hands clapping—
the destiny of strangers is chalk.

I.

We move
with birds, with fish
arrayed on a surface, touched
by space between us.
Perfect alone, we seek completion.
A leaf falls anyway
in time, in anticipation.
The complexity of one moves me.

A new arrangement presses up;
we go south, cold into heat.
Here color is abstract, your hair
a version of itself
in chambers full of that moon white.
Something happens among men, fish, virgins.

An island rain.
Wind the same temperature as air,
a slow endurance of gray
eased to the sea
where change ends in repetition.
A wave hesitates before it releases;
silence: the core of love being made.

She said, "Wait.
There are strangers inside.
Eagles gather where the body is."
She said, "I thought of you, dreaming her."
Her lover is my lover, the one
who taught the exclusivity of being loved.

Between timidity and terror
the body's star sings.
It is impossible to charm
a snail from its shell.
I am full of emergencies.

Wait, wait.
Strangers are exclusive.
Inside eagles gather
to dream her, one her, one lover.
I thought of being loved.
She who taught said,
"Where the body is."

What is the fever of roses, the
delirium of gold? He died playing tennis;
she was kissed by a bird.
A flat room, a painting, intrudes.
A red stain veils space,
holding it up. A residue of seeing
frame within frame within us.
The edge is our signature.

A breach. You go on alone.
I am making doodles on spare paper
thinking of a barracuda, how I write
as an excuse to smoke in the morning.
These filters in the square ashtray,
Happy Birthday written all over it,
are the size and shape of those corals
you picked off the beach to make necklaces.
I wish you could see things more plainly.

A new arrangement moves up.
We press south. The colors are heat,
a version of white, that moon white.
Something is absent among us.
The painting is *L'Atelier Rouge*.

Wednesday.
Something invisible where nothing is.
Dark lines above and below.
A green goblet full of chalks
ready to mark the seam between us;
walls are pitted with holes
where pictures hung:
something impaled, nailed between us.

Your thighs I can draw.
They drew mine apart.
Curves, but in fact
only these, only yours.

Fragments on the shore are alike,
bred of the sea's indifference.
I wake with one leg raised, a finger
on my life. She rips open the curtains,
she's stiff. We are in a room
with a man with a paintbrush and a horse.
And father, the cause of all journeys we take.
And mother, so lost, only the sea
under the moon catches her back.

The room insists on itself.
What is see-through cannot be seen.
Shallow breaths, waiting for the birth.

II.

The new closes out the old.
I am reading as snow flurries
Monday, in February, in a
hot, dry room.
The days are slippery,
too difficult for make-believe.

You tie
my arms behind my back
with the red velvet belt
from my robe.
I love feeling helpless;
I am not.
I am tired, I sleep.
You go away, an image.

Is this it, this familiarity with nothing?

Each day you appear.
You come to let me know
you do not want me. You come
to see I know you do not want me.
You come to witness your absence.
You come to maintain the irresolute.
You come just in case, to inhabit us.

The white egret on the rock
stands before you,
afraid and unknown.
It is beautiful to itself
when it flies, as I am, alone.

Mid-afternoon. Pulled asleep
by a squat figure with no hair.
It wants to tell me something secret.
Questions are raised; I'm speechless.
Now it rises from a chair and begins.
It's an old story about a sea-goddess
who turns men into fish
and feeds them on virgins.

And you dream too,
thrust awake by your voice
howling for mercy, stretched
for the tail of a spirit.

An agenda comes towards us
in disguised events,
distorted with scrappy intimacies.
I'll steal if I have to.

Her lover returns.
This is the end of the story.
Tomorrow she waits again
and so forth. The situation
is as it is, for each of us.

III.

Far west at the city's coast
windy and cold and trucks
still luminous under the highway.
At a crossing of lights you ask,
"Where are you?" Here, answering.
A series of mirrors shields us;
I look into you at the landscape behind me.

All journeys are alike, all cause.
We take father, mother, a man
with a paintbrush and a horse.
We are born with one leg raised.
A man with fragments is lost.
My finger is stiff, it rips her back.
Curtains catch on the shore;
a white indifference is in the room.

The moon scales down. Rain
or spit follows a tensile route.
A catastrophe of trees, of bald women
arguing with birds
in a wind that tongues their faces
with a watery event that moves towards them
as they move towards it.

Another night with you is more than I can stand.
Events trespass; dreams I forget.

Today
how your tongue in my imagination
tastes as real
as window light
cast on the veins of your arms.
I cannot retrieve what does not occur.

I wake,
my right eye swollen
with smoke in the blood.
Disoriented, I steer to the kitchen.
Something catches fire.
Water is loose on the slate black floor.

Flames
up in flames in orange smoke,
an emergency of change. Figurines
on the mantelpiece melt
and the fat sculpture
seated on the bookcase
flees its curves
as the old season gives up its ghost.

IV.

At last you wanted to drop everything and stand perfectly
still as if waiting, patiently waiting, not for someone to take
you away from all this to a house on a hill, a remote cabin
heated only by natural fire, lit only by natural light and filled
with the silence of long-standing knowledge; not for this
perennial savoir-savior who haunts all your best moments
with the expectation of more to come

The arrival of winter is chalk

After many mornings of this passive stance, this stillness
which allowed the events to move against you as they would,
either by accident or design, until it was impossible to tell
one from the other except as a matter of course, sunrise to
sunset, you would become acquainted with the minute details
of a bird's flight, with the moments when the wind died
down, as you had seen sailors anticipate a wave in the water
surface; but easy, also, with the unexpected:

Come home your house is on fire.
Come home your father is dying.
Come home your child is lost.
Come home your mother is mad.
Come home your son has crashed.
Come home your lover is dead.

As it happens, you could not go back into the progression,
into the slow movement and the rapid accumulating phrases
which lead finally to a climax which sent you into a delirium
of relief; nor could you retreat to the clearing in the woods,
nor to the first room from which you had escaped.

Dumb cathedral
forget it sweetheart, dreamer,
last princess in a cardboard tower.
The cross warns of deceit and hesitation.
Your illusions make me weep.
Alone in a forest? Whose crumbs?
Your brother has gone on into new fables.
He's wearing a red scarf,
he is the cardinal in the tree.

Things became remote, and began to resemble each other so
that the opening became an act of will, a clearing of spaces
quite literally. Having collected such a mess of odd posses-
sions, such an inheritance, it was now a matter of exclusion
and this you found to be a thing imagined, a landscape of
snow on which was written something formal in a handwrit-
ing you could not recognize as belonging to anyone

Type set
the trees cast across the line of sight
in long prose rhythms.

Still you wanted to run backwards into a terrible fast
rewinding, back before the leaving, before time came out of
the grass onto the open road, before your instinct to trust
a flower to live faded in you so you knew all expectation
ended in lost desire; back to the shoals where you stood by
the rapids watching the water fall through itself as if there
were no surface

The thing recalled is chalk

A compendium of images you had dragged with you from
island to island, ignoring the bleak danger of arrival but
living in fear of going back to find the one person who kept
your secret had left no further address so you were left with
these few articles of presence: a letter from California, a
key, a blue sweater, and all those lyrics which would from
now on transport you into the dull separation which you had
unwittingly provoked

The destiny of strangers is chalk

v.

On the other side of the mountain
nothing changed; only the old had aged.
We scour the view for details, stalk rooms,
count spoons. New leaves
lit with the same old greens, the same
population of windows offsets distance.
A still life, restored by washing panes.

How do we accomplish it?
Is familiarity nothing?
Sunday is made of clouds which endure,
hanging on Sundays. You say, "I fade,
getting old. You go on and on.
If only," you say, "you knew what you want."

A child swings in the graveyard
of the church, a replica
of misremembered verse.
The roses look French, too exact.
Days lengthen into twilight Magrittes.

Space dilates, contracts.
We shout across interims
but the body takes on a new shape
in strange hands. We are
constantly at risk, constantly enfolded.

I swim to the horizon.
Watching from the shore you
cannot tell how far, if I move or not.
The waves touch your feet.
To this extent we are not separate.

Wet, tight, I return,
my hands cupped with glittering shells
for the aquarium. I explain.
All space is private, detached.
These are intimate details in focus,
ideas of the actual, longings met.
My body is my address; here I am.
The view from the window is the same.

I explain.
My body, my hands, here.
All I return is private, detached.
The aquarium is in focus,
set with tight shells.
All details are intimate.
My address is a view from the window, glittering.

Do not come at me like an eagle on the fly.
I know what the mountain is.
She goes back for a visit.
The apples are heavy on the trees.
An offering is made but she refuses
and runs across a bridge.
In the morning she yields,
is given fresh water, first light.

I would lean on you now, were you around.
These sporadic days reduce me to new,
wanting to unwrap, to be surprised.
She said, "As if you were always on the verge,
negotiating between, and the rocks slide
and you are nowhere again." And he,
"You must proceed to ecstasy or quit."

The dark moves to be met.
Fear makes noises from wings, close
overhead. There is no repetition.
She surrenders to it.
But you say nothing, dealing images.
Not now, but you said it once, a choice
that placed us at this table distance.
When I am old, I will need to dream.
Remember I do not intend to forget.

Having walked out into the night to find the stone as moist
and brilliant as the lilies on the pond she knew the entrance
had, after all, been made; that she had gone behind the screen
with the landscape stitched on it, beyond the full moon, the
ocean, and the hill leading to the house into the darkness
which was illuminated from an altogether different source:

Something invisible, dark, green, pitted.
Something with holes.
Something where pictures hung.
Something between us.
Something above and below.
Something ready to mark.
A full goblet. Wednesday. Chalk.

Late evening.
The delicate aspect of the day
has waited until the last minute,
leaving us with only a capacity for sadness.
Nothing specific, at least not yet.
A tune has formed around some sort of Chopin waltz
that cheats its way through melancholy.

But still, with all this gloom
a grasshopper is staring at the sun
in some garden where a young man asks:
"Dr. Panza, where are your roses?"
In England, for instance, where distinctions
are made.
        The dim notes play
and the dim stars shine more than usual.
Does a crowd always gather?
This very afternoon, a woman lay on the sidewalk.

Standing at a Distance

We take the last off the counter and now, the counter
clear, begin. She stands to one side, her
blue sleeves indicating the moment: she's brighter
than before. He keeps steady, he may be an umpire or
the captain of a ship. They are cut-out, austere.
I think they must pass through me to endure
although I am neither ready nor
capacious.
        She goes first, aware
of sloped light over chairs on the porch where
the dense continuation is a marriage. His eye
rests easily on nothing; where nothing meets.
She knows the low winter sun will touch three apples.
I am upstairs in front of a long, wood-framed glass.
The branches cast branches. He soon will appear
walking across the grass towards the dim solarium.
The white towels lift in the wind, causing triangles.

It was a soulless, faded time.
The radical fringe was no more
than a whisper in Grandma's ear and all
the astute and caring folk had shut themselves in
for the winter, when some old longing
crept among them like smoke in autumn leaves
making everything once again pertinent.
Uncle Bill was alarmed and Aunt Pris
dreamed that night of something genuine.
"This is no time for flags," proclaimed their son
at breakfast, and so it was not.
In the distance they could hear the sound
of spokes, as if the old windmill
on Main Street had started, after all these years, up.

Something slips through the element of truth
and tosses like a seed in a cardboard box.
The Chinese fiancé did not show up
but the alcoholic painter does
by just applying himself to non-stop work.
For three years they slept back to back.
She learned to tell lies; he
believes the pain is in his head, not his life.

You can't walk through the streets all fuzzed up.
The day flickers unsteadily in a paper cup.
I'm not used to the lines which leave things out
and this slide through seasons is arduous and slow.
The process of waking hurts, the way
dreams have a habit of your name or your face.
Somewhere, outside city limits, a habit of flowers
is getting under way. The scarf is light; the earth moist.

Desdemona, whose name comes to mind
like the taste of pineapple, steps through
the door in her torn skirt and looks up.
"Still raining." As it turns out
this is a slipshod universe, not
the opulent crystal chandelier
she ordered from Tiffany for the diningroom.
Bricks fall down the shaft
of things in general, to turn up
a day later in a book of photographs.
Her heart is permanently overcast.
She will need to wear a coat until a new age
dawns, its light filtered like charm
through a crowded, uncomfortable room.
She'll move on. A marriage will take place
although by then her looks will have changed
as well as her character. She'll slide
down the banister, all smiles, all dressed up.

But the temperature dipped unexpectedly.
These inner states can be dangerous, even
with soft focus so they flare
after spending hours and hours in bed
or tucked under a log in the wet woodlands.
The toadstools are smooth and taut and sudden
although motionless, unlike
the gong or the owl.
                    What about these bricks?
What about history? Why is it far off
when it should be close, as if
someone had clipped the foreground
and our ears ring with a high-pitched note?
Perhaps because the war has ended
and emergencies sprout in strange places:
under the bed, in brown paper bags, at home.

Perhaps none of us ever believed
contemplating the acute world would rescue us
from it. Between frequency and absence
a world is missing in action, although
one is still friends with the bride. Lying
in bed, he proposes a new form of separation
and she accepts, feeling already radiant.
The song of praise from Catalonia
is energetic and glad as your niece
who is fourteen and no longer a virgin.

Barcelona is beautiful. I know
of a beautiful girl named Gloria Barcelona.
Once I thought there were instances of magic
until a philosopher friend, now dead, said
it was pure coincidence. He pretended to be
dying of cancer, then killed himself.
An acquaintance wrote me the news on brown paper.
He left me his books, which I never got, but just
the other day you said: "The world is all that is the case."

The ferry goes back and forth across the waters;
we are thirty miles at sea. She says,
"An elongated merlin on the roof top," not meaning
a bird, but a man who is. It rises, the heated air,
the light, dispersed by gulls overhead, and fear
that she might have been there:
walking the widow's walk.
                              She dressed for the occasion:
the image precursing, outlined on an extended pier
where she watched the man with his bride, a girl.
The tide is not easy to know; the fog unfathomable.
"If the sound of warning stops we are surely in danger."
Somehow the masts, reappearing, are too magical
or too real, a spray of wild wands below her view.
Their immanence, the sail, is a measure of will. Silence
passes silence. The decision to leave invades the harbor.

Minimum procedure. Last ditch. Greyhound.
Flaws stiff in bad weather and grace
less roads in little running things without means
because and because. Either hide or seek.
It is the wrong night, this blue one, notes
troubling at the window, stretched
across a chord, fingers, keys pressed down
and falling salt and pepper. Now scan
the invention. Same old trip. Tunes
in the wake. No way to rearrange this arrangement.
Perfected form. Ding. Dung. Slight sway,
slight hedge. A breeze to clear the air.
Ask nothing, ask nothing. Or please
in the rainy season. Or dry up. Beggars.
How about making a habit out of it?
But chant loud when the tired bird flies up.

May I get you something? The cook's out
and Marie the blond ice-skating champ
is dancing on skates under a luminous twig.
Neat thighs. Later on we'll tell stories.
She's curling, she's all smoke and slow
moving back against the green evergreens.
Stand back. Make me another. Anything unclear
is unwanted. This is precision tuning. This
is the fork. This is the whole encapsuled.
This is the daring trapeze. Don't ardent
and don't tinker with sorry, sorry. Each
of us is going somewhere else. And you?
Who wants to know? Off to the forest with
the ice queen for a rest. Give my regards
to that talented young man with a knack for gifts.

So much for this morning to be the next. Plain
space. Fields in the vicinity, but why not not?
To whom must I speak in the long line of favors?
Who here votes? Questions at the edge of sheets.
One big scribble in the notes. You coming with me?
No. You going? Yes, thought I might go on up
on out on on. Flash art. Snazzy polaroid shot.
Teatime. I'm just finishing up. Be right with you.
Is bitter and sweet at once for your sister's sake.
Remember Ophelia remembering? Here's this for that;
here's that for this. I got stems of winter flowers
and some seed. I tender kindness gentle caring loving.
Tit for that. You like? You want? Go to Egypt.
Find Leonardo the chemist. He makes ceremonies.

January Hill

in memory of Matthew Carlebach

To recall you pleases nothing to think about: you
cannot be recalled. Halfway there, this transpires
and nothing remains. Bargain for what? You said
"Do not hope" and then a mere glib of your hand
with no sequence. I'll kill the next brother
who loves me. Back here, nothing but stick trees,
pantomime, and fear of forever.
I want to tread dangerously on anything that moves.

Your father will sleep through it, a vestige. But
the farewell is more than curtains
and a fit of stardom, isn't it? Not even sight
illumines the situation. Kidnapped, sliced, a whiff
of fume and pretty soon I say "I love you" out loud.
Here we are: piss-drenched snow, the wallowing,
the stretch of bitch cold obliterating all but necessity.
The pigs will be slain. By then the trick is known:
to invoke, repeat, insinuate your name into each day;
day, in this case, endurance. We jump the fence.
It is tomorrow. The slaughter was brilliant but
the trees stay against the hill which, in summer, is gone.

The Day After

An island is not a window onto a broad climate
but a caption describing what is beyond
and illegible. The tides are high,
the light rivets and we are aware
of an intrinsic mode less probable than music.
The sound is the pitch of a shell, a brilliance
that parades before us as if we were marooned
in some incessant necessary garden
or an ancient resort furnished with intimacies.
By now the moon does not count as the moon
slips out of sight into the abstract, the luminous.

There are no vertical landscapes, just
a low, monotonous museum lit from within by
other, giant lights. The windows are shuttered.
By the time we arrive it is too late
and we know why some houses seem blind and others
merely logical. We cannot intrude on these limits;
even the dunes are the occasion of dull enterprise.
The fires, for instance. How many are deliberately set?
Last winter's snow was sobering: she walked across
in a purple coat and the birds were held down, pecking.

There never was a gate, although it seemed possible
to walk through to where the farm may have been.
A platter of flowers had been brought in
and I had continued to sleep
enclosed by rain fencing the distance.
The animals had all been painted into the landscape
and everyone was tired of invention; tired, even,
of the sort of thing that stares you in the face
dull with hunger.
                         Halfway across the field we stopped.
There was no way to be admitted, despite
the fact that we would be known on sight.
What lie would I tell? Sometimes the provocation
made me giddy, and I flirted around the periphery
just outside the frame where air gets at the edges,
raking oblivion. I woke up aware
that the whole night had been spent
in trivial but terrifying proximities: someone had said
"wipe your nose" and someone else had hated the plates.
The month had changed overnight: now
the season would not let go, the air stubborn and clear
and cold, like an invitation to definition.
But some things had become impossible. It was impossible
to waltz or to sew on buttons. We could, however,
move out of the house into a tent
with a very old doll, and nobody would stare, or wave so long.

_____ September Solitaire _____

There are always added difficulties: unwashed glasses,
the box with some sweaters, the floral arrangement
in the kitchen, the kitchen floor. It was a grid
of pale blue and gray linoleum; it no longer exists.
All of us move in time for winter.
Things are most dangerous when habits are kicked;
birds, and the way you imagine.
                                        We tell stories.
This to restrain the sense that we would give in
too easily when the time came. The time had come.
The first red and the first green are not the same;
between death and birth are radical colors,
of which the trees are stain. I told stories for hours,
each made from imminent, rendered places; talk itself
a terrain. I recall games: ducking and kisses and tails.
Someone is always blinded. Someone was removed in a chair.

They buzz air, they stay above in lit races
where ambulances are silent. They
freely associate and amend résumés
with tidings of terror, construed loosely
on tight hips.
              They love something smooth,
hand-painted: *fleurs* enameled on tin,
old ivory, any old thing to keep things in.
They will gather nothing to them but rooms
to zero in on leaving: the long hall out.
In stealing the breeze, they
leave us in Miami with too many red blooms
and statements both contrary and vague
in attitudes of stiff chagrin, like
statues of war heroes in memorial parks.
They are enhanced by weather; we are stuck with it.

So what if majesty has been sold? It is
inoperative anyway, under the weight
of its latest rendition, the gold barely visible,
inside, under the closed flap.
Besides, this son and daughter business
has altered, with costumes more various
than the names of gods and goddesses.
Diana hunts and is hunted by her father,
whose trident is in the bank.
She still sees everything; nothing escapes.
As for the other sister, she
is in love with the boy at the racetrack.
Her father sold peaches at the A&P
and sat on a ladder in the kitchen drinking beer.
So much for kings, and as for the princess
in the garden, she gave birth to seven sons,
only one of which survived. A waste of strength,
all those heavy months at the end of summer
when the nursery was repainted blue or pink.
The surviving son plays the organ at the local church.

Under the surface. Crocodiles rise from a slow,
tentative gauze; lacuna of friendship endured;
gathering moss. Insistence, less than necessary,
one way out of mole-infested holidays, the whole
moving in with obsession and enterprise. I
don't believe in that stuff. Magic objects,
metaphysic, esthetic of right form, these
slim approximations from the pages of books.
What use? What's the? That, then. Our
professor had aged. We were as certain as orchards.

Multiple choice. Choose one of the above.
Was Psyche embraced by none-other-than Love?
Eros. Amour. A mass. Erase. Each answer
more tedious than the last, dubbing in for hours,
the scene cut tighter than the script. Poetic
license. He said, "I just want to get close."
You are. Venturing too far, he quotes
a new degree of insight while you eye the lilies
on the ashtray slyly. "Don't predict. What
you intuit cannot be exchanged on the open market."

The story of a life. It has peaked, the
natural romance, in a myth through swinging doors:
a tall lean man named Dakota, so exotic in New York.
Pressure of disguise breeds a strain of exaltation.
The Twin Towers rise like wet fish
and as briefly tragic. Your ex-lover is impressed:
you are free of attachments. He says the essence
of abstraction is human or the abstract is
human essence, I forget which, and paints your
portrait suspended on a sofa above Times Square lights.

This nineteenth-century stool is residual speech;
the blue vase from Paris: allure of image.
Then whom do you admire? O, mother and father,
various wild beasts of the realm. And what
do you fear? Cold discovered under
the enchanted ruse, a mummy in the temple
mute and intractable. Chopping ice for fuel.
The true dark thins, dumping favorite themes
over the edge as we lose our grip. History,
into an aftermath of kith and strangers, delivers.

The disappointment of an unripe fruit, thoughtless
curves in summer. Somewhere the mind
springs to action, a spare equilibrium
culled from the sensuality of the moment, no more
abstract than touch, which is. A technique is present
even with desire: to disperse
the tight arrangements which gang up in love
and war. We are so easily soothed by details,
even the handwritten page of coded, delicate meanings
gives definition when all else fails, and all else does.

Untitled Seascape

The list of titles has exceeded its limits.
Now each word emerges hedging its bets
with vernacular, or the turtle
stranded on its back where kids left it,
soft grid telling of slow passage close to earth.
The urge to break out comes
just as fatigue takes over, each of us not ready,
in dread of another festivity, as yet untitled.
It is the collector who collects
porcelain birds to place on the mantel
above inlaid tiles, while real birds exact
white fiestas from dark clouds.
We are walking along the beach as if
nothing could be analyzed, at least not how,
with each step, our capacity to cause each other
harm is stalled in its tracks
and in the tracks of the capricious, now
the list of titles has exceeded its limits.

Romance

She said nothing; he mentioned his daughter.
They met, one evening, in a room without coercion
and from there digressed to a place
remote as a park and as wandering: grass
littered with small defects, fountains waterless.
They forgot their hobbies and skipped out on
real appointments with friends. Hair, mouth, skin.
They knew them, perched on a limb each morning, singing.

He despised summer, the risky season, melodious,
thick air entangled air netting journeys he dreamed of;
choice itself a violence. He craved
an immune but legible haven where he might raise himself
to Kingdom Come. He lay in bed, her face
overhead, obliterating: a Byzantine portrait.
He mentioned his daughter: "Everyone starts with image,
clutching the long white doll that precedes illusion."

She said nothing, searched the attic for clues.
The old pictures stabbed, vindictive, private:
someone standing by a fence in front of a garden.
She came across letters irrevocably folded
and dreamed they were a shape tangible in space, of
huge porcelains cast at her feet by an entirely white man.
She sent a grave wind to molest him; he vanished.
Each moment jettisoned desire until they were wicked with loss.

A longer, unfurled space
might meander further and further from reach;
the whole concept of "rooms" laid
in flattened imitations: a lawn of walls,
shelves, hooks; carpets repeating patterns in
grass, keys locked in rocks, an upholstered foliage.
No reference. A cool continuum of things
easy and meaningless, an infinite peeling of paint,
a casual loss.
   This method is one of fading, of
hanging out days on end into the sun until
fabric lets go of substance and light is remnant.

A Visit to the Country

There are legends which please the inner ear,
that part that yearns, does not hear
but knows when the mechanical rabbit is slain
by the real thing. The real thing
revokes the vulgar indiscriminate corpse
into pain of birth, told and retold
by the woman who otherwise does not speak.

She stops drinking and digs holes for roses.
One is called Chicago Peace, bred
to resemble the white rose on the tapestry
in which the unicorn distills myth from history.
She thinks of Saint Francis as the bluebirds nest
in a small wood box. They exist, but
Saint Francis is a reverie among bald, silent monks.
On an island in the pond two turtles shine.
They wait centuries for the geese to lay.

I called three flying geese herons, confused
between long legs and long necks.
I know the difference between women and birds.
But neither of us knows why
butterflies fly at the sea and die there,
intact and closed.
                 The subject eludes, not the words.
They are rinsed into irradiant puddles
where the sky leaks light onto pavements
and the trees are flat. And as we follow the slippage
we see how scale counts and that deep in the shine
of the perceived landscape is a chain of events
like a handcuff of stars; or pebbles.
My mother always looked away, out of the picture.
And I am known for decorous deceits
from which neither bruise nor wailing comes,
just refusal to observe the perishing.
I know there is loss in the heavens even if,
fixed on enchantment, I stare only at colors
abridged from history and from the history of awe.

Since then we have taken to gazing out the window.
Bricks span octaves, light
speeds up to dare the clandestine opera to begin.
It is just before day. Matilda, asleep,
dreams she is in a room among plants
and wives who say nothing but sit.
The strings suggest glass, a stroll down the beach.
A tall man enters stage left, led by the tune of the oboe.
Matilda is dancing.
                          And so the imagined world
changes the imagined world with a new set.
We tear down walls, pull nails
easily from old wood. You say:
"I care more for the snow outdoors
than for your spoons, forks, and heart."
This is a memorable winter: more than the usual
share of storms. And so Matilda wakes.
Outside it really snows harsh as desire and as
particular, its fine scrim everywhere.
We take to gazing out the window
while drips drip down the far river and its
turn out of sight. The wide view causes this account:
hovering, low, the river is still, verging on scenery.
Things come down from above, from nowhere,
the sky white and impacted where the river cuts across.
He paints from behind his back,
eliminating details as from a great distance.
This is a form of loss, a reduced portrait.
There is a dark gray recess in a dark gray recess.
There are small heaps of snow hidden from wind and sun.

The song, invisible, prolongs, but passage is colorless
and, although we are reminded that silence is golden,
goes unnoticed. The day has its moments.
Even with the hovering of gray antecedents,
heavy with causation, we
arch back, away from the sheen of declaration to where
the wall must curve and further curve until it too
is a cloud.
                   What's wrong with decoration? Why not make
these lush impressions lush, and swoon
as the green barge passes to change everything but the weather
which no longer counts? A cold wet Thursday: that's exact.
The sky is a shaft of steady fragmentation
through which the barge must pass as if forever downward to sea.
Elaborate, yes, but is it slow or fast? Silence is fast;
it quickens absence. Sooner or later it arrives, as you arrive,
caused by procedure. The clouds, the chairs, the barge
(the chairs are covered with a terrible orange), all
are objects which subside as the mind interferes
with its recourse: language causes you: you must be declared.
It rained all day without you but with a candor that is resolute.

Many Times, But Then

It hardly seems possible. Between yellow chairs
and leaves about to fall, the volume
just high enough to disturb the otherwise settled air
into Mozartian expertise and your eyes
that have so many times
touched my heart. The vacancies are rare.
And I have said so many times, but then
here we are just as the sea is preparing for winter.
What days have come have gone
and today is the anniversary of someone's death
but then I am familiar with things that pass
even as the sun flares descending, an image
for which cathedrals have been made, glass cut
to let it in.
          There is a gradual lessening
where light is peeling off the walls onto the floor.
A small painted table by the bed.
Are we stranded in here? You said
we must live in the world and in the poem, but then
he left home and she is going mad, her
eminent sadness stiff as flowers held in a vase too long.
From time to time I lose you in the glare
of a blue robe in summer but then the window has me
kneeling to see. The birds masquerade as song;
the leaves, futile and passionate, abstract gold from green.

We had spent days, maybe months, in the hopes
the irresolute would yield alternates; had met, secretly,
to offset the density which is haphazard and unaccountable
as the sky. The insular, narrow passage of a room
had been replaced by another margin, held
in the flat gaze of a mirror image.
Had it been a parade we would have noticed something.
But things are hardly ever in place, even
the crowd of trees at the lawn's edge
leans as if to follow the light which will not land
anywhere that light falls.
                              And yet, the meadow is alert
with yellow tropes like some moments dropped on the fly.
The nights speak for themselves: splendid, aloof.
The sky disembarks, to be resumed in a particular light
we did not choose to watch. It carries towards us
a sense that we know the rest: the dim, still incipience.

The Green Scarf

An old incentive, somewhat like evening but less
guarded, got me here. At what cost?
How do I cast out "forever" and "always"
which come as an old green
that seems to spread with the twilight?
There is a cling in the air now as I watch
you go towards solitude, where you find solace
in attention to dread. But I am also
lapsing, because today is a scarf
made of silk and silk, as you know, perishes.
The one my mother had I now have: it is emerald.
Just above the hem it frays, becomes less and less
until it is not.
            I am not good at guesswork.
Last year I knew more than this;
yesterday I was better at today than now,
which folds in on itself like a scarf
in an open drawer of the small white table
that was always by her bed. This morning,
in a dream, we danced, suspended in air.
I know that absence is a form of holding, as love is.

Reynolda Gardens

For some time we thought it possible to wander,
to let our grip on the inevitable
loosen, so that we could
stroll round to a new perspective:
this formal garden open to the public.
Standing just above on the slope
it looks like madness, an invitation
to impossible choices and unbearable nearness.
Yellow, pale pink, white, scarlet,
each an aspect of itself,
each named, each immune to mimic
although the scent is of a lucid, indelible type.

A calm had come into focus,
a real but frail version of what was wanted—
not defined, framing no image—
but imagined nevertheless like the end of a sentence.
We had reached the point of arrival
when loss drops off
in a generous show of moments
for which there is no recovery.
We walked through unaware of surprise: we were it.
It had the effect of an embrace
reflected in huge, locked windows facing the gardens.

What caused a musical persuasion and what
gained entrance was at first
limited: an alteration in the span
of the gradual. We could not yet fix a name.
And in not fixing a name, we went ahead
with a sense of pages turning
and of music getting lost on arrival.
The rain, lasting, helped
as if it were a mention, a sign of its effect
allowed by what we knew all during:
that it would also not rain and we would know it.
We were on an excursion,
that was clear, but
we did not dare to take anything along
even though we stopped from time to time
to make a presentation: "I give you this."
This was something we had given before
and therefore had an emptiness
or a pause in substance but we could not do
otherwise, given the extent
of what had gone before: the formal part.
The inclusions were drenched but discrete.
We had learned to hear it note by note
and to arrive, perilous but glad, at the disclosed.

Gramercy Park Evening

I am, in these instances, aware
there is much to be desired, much left to desire,
and the rest abided. The late hour has everything
turned down; even the constant fleet of wheels
is another noise: less. I was trying to sleep
and to imagine us near the sea, the light
skinny and unhedged, the sea
a ribbed plate, a wide blue absolute
into which pink is introduced like an idea in music.

Desire is an aspect of ethics; belief is not.
You can move a peach across the table
without changing its color but the light, this light,
casts a shadow of doubt. What we perceive
is part dream, part deceit; what we want
touches knowledge. The park is something you
could not know about: late afternoon, a walk,
the walk I sometimes took towards a cadence
of real images: the gate, the grass, the lock.
There was a sense that things are lit
from within, of high, shut carriages and women in hats.

Chappaqua Reverie

I.

Gauguin at the river not thinking limbs, green, anything.
No landscape fully explained, raw ingredients
sliced into radiant details and talk
of Iceland moss. Prepare the dark for dark.
Goaded all night by splash, packed with perishables
and carted through a roomy museum. Water, glass,
the faint aroma of berries. Clarity is not swift.
A bird needs leverage for wing-span, lift.

Tiny blue tiles laid in white. We are
translating ourselves but indigenous as the blue
in Cadaques. House. Tree. Mother and father.
Mountain. Sun. Me. If I am going
where am I going? Still forward, still back.
Rectangle after rectangle. Do not step.
Horizon or entrance.
                    I am upstairs again, have
waded through scent to the dowager in wallpaper,
through soap and moth and forsythia. She
is withered, mysterious. I sit on the bed
with a detached retinue of perceptions,
isolations of fury and origin. Her father,
her father's father, her father's father's father.
Her sister. Her sister's son. Her sister's son's wife.
Who died first? Her daughter my mother their cousin your sister.

II.

What do I see? What do I see? Owls, others, each
word flinging towards a sunset
where even the gray fox hurries to meet his fictions.
Pretty lies on the horizon; hammock sways.
Big gets bigger gets plastered on the moon.
Where wind begins. Out of the stagnant. Snails
shoot darts, a slow ordeal in summer. Gold
smothers rose and spur for a peppercorn rent.
We meet in a room called Rome, sleep in France
with jewels and old portraits. Lapsed saint, syntax.
Closed in event, the only school a miracle of
loves and wishes, we hike to the foot of Annapurna,
white upheaval of magnificent.
                    Calling you up.
I see siblings and sibyls at night writing taboos
on subway cars. Large ladies drink loud talk
of our mystery, finding it out. Sib, sib. Kiss.
Form takes the form of disguise; style flourishes.
How many words a rose, but named in Latin not romance.
Only the owl knows the worth of an owl. Raised on city,
who sleeps? Rust is refusal. How can we embrace?
We did not dream for three nights, or touch.
The apricot, the brocade, stars fly out
stinging our capacity to see. I have no recollection.
A great aunt in a hotel room with a nurse, pink arrangements.

The Yellow Linen Dress

in memory of Elisabeth Wardwell Lauterbach

1.

A solemn discourse is not necessary
although I am inclined
to triumph and exalted states
that remind me of mother at her best,
how everything about her was sheer.
This is my habit: to come through
vanity—through her—
and to sweep away the ribbons
she shed as she sailed into image.
She had a ring around her, but was not religious.

2.

The miraculous is no more than what
comes naturally after
cold weather: this large hat
and these motherhoods
that glide to an early stop on the boulevard.
Her best was fugal: she moved
from place to place and then went back
to pick the inevitable.
I stopped bothering after a while,
leaving her to impinge on her garden.

3.

He waits for her to arrive
in the family carriage.
He has heard she has beautiful hair
that she pins at her neck like a cloud.
He wears his white suit and straw hat.
He thinks the rich have bad taste
but is unsure, ambitious at heart.
The carriage arrives; she turns her head.
He thinks he will marry her, take her
on his boat, his incertitude.

4.

Rain on the lawn falls softly,
softly falling, the falling rain.
I begin to see how mannered feelings are,
dispatched to the eye of the beholder.
"I turned my head to show
how beautiful my hair is.
He stood on the porch and thought
he would marry me. We sailed away
on his boat. I sat on the deck
and watched the sun rise. It was ugly and pink."

5.

A birdless sky, seadawn, one lone star,
is what she saw
as she sat on deck while he slept below.
She thought it was disgusting.
They had five daughters and now
she reads the same book over and over.
It gives her solace; she hates surprises.
Her daughter ran off and turned into ashes.
I sit on the bed. We talk of the weather.
Her hair is pinned to her neck like a cloud.

6.

I sit on the bed.
The ashes have been dumped at sea.
I have come back as part of the estate.
We do not mention the flutter
that hurries late summer into fall
or name the departed.
We will not name the departure, as
a leaf among many. She feeds the birds
at breakfast, her hair
a cloud full of mild and muttering rain.

7.

Her daughter wore a linen dress and
pearls. She sat for her portrait.
She turned her head to show
how the eye of the beholder is
forgotten. I came back
too late: she had turned into ashes.
I sat on the bed and thought:
I am going to sink her, softly, softly,
sink her. And as soon as the rain falls,
forget her. We talked of the weather.

8.

The temptation is to shred it,
to tear it to ribbons.
Otherwise it is her father's boat
and I write to articulate
the drift of smoke between her fingers.
She was the occasion of weather,
her mother's hair full of rain.
Her surface vanished, leaving a profile.
He stood on the porch behind the gate.
She followed the inhibited ferry.

9.

Everything is hers: she went through it.
She played at the gate, fearful.
She made solemn flight
in the absence of a father.
She could lie. She could write
with lips, eyes, hair,
and the way she did it
indicated how I was to follow,
how the sequel to her would be discourse
made from an inhibited, necessary image.

Gardenia

There is "corduroy" and there is "long brown hair"
and they could be the beginning.
After all it helps,
if you describe, to make the tactile real.
Then there is the precinct of "crave,"
how it goes down and stays down
like an anchor to longing
and the pulleys on which the pail ascends
chafe against the mildew and the rock.
If I give you "crave"
will you trade
water running in the sink
where I placed the gardenia?